CONTENTS

CHOICE
Jericho Brown • *The Tradition* • Picador

RECOMMENDATIONS
Anthony Anaxagorou • *After the Formalities* • Penned in the Margins
Mary Jean Chan • *Flèche* • Faber
Seni Seneviratne • *Unknown Soldier* • Peepal Tree Press
Peter Sirr • *The Gravity Wave* • The Gallery Press

SPECIAL COMMENDATION
Carmen Bugan • *Lilies from America: New & Selected Poems* • Shearsman

RECOMMENDED TRANSLATION
Manuel Forcano • *Maps of Desire* • Translated by Anna Crowe • Arc Publications

PAMPHLET CHOICE
Scott McKendry • *Curfuffle* • The Lifeboat

WILD CARD
Dunya Mikhail • *In Her Feminine Sign* • Carcanet Press

REVIEWS

LISTINGS

Poetry Book Society

CHOICE SELECTORS RECOMMENDATION SPECIAL COMMENDATION	SANDEEP PARMAR & VIDYAN RAVINTHIRAN
TRANSLATION SELECTOR	GEORGE SZIRTES
PAMPHLET SELECTORS	A.B. JACKSON & DEGNA STONE
WILD CARD SELECTOR	ANTHONY ANAXAGOROU
CONTRIBUTORS	SOPHIE O'NEILL NATHANIEL SPAIN OISIN POWER JULIA McGEE-RUSSELL
EDITORIAL & DESIGN	ALICE KATE MULLEN

Membership Options
Associate 4 *Bulletins* a year (UK £22, Europe £35, Rest of the World £42)
Full 4 Choice books and 4 *Bulletins* a year (£55, £65, £75)
Charter 20 books and 4 *Bulletins* (£180, £210, £235)
Education 4 books, 4 *Bulletins*, posters, teaching notes (£79, £89, £99)
Charter Education 20 books, 4 *Bulletins*, posters, teaching notes (£209, £245, £275)
Translation 4 Translation books and 4 *Bulletins* (£65, £90, £99)
Student 4 Choice books and 4 *Bulletins* (£35, £55, £65)
Translation Plus Full 4 Choices, 4 *Bulletins* & 4 Translation books (£98, £120, £132)
Translation Plus Charter 20 books, 4 *Bulletins* & 4 Translation books (£223, £265, £292)
Single copies £6
Cover Art Photograph by Zied Mnif **Website** www.snapwi.re/user/zmnif/photos
Copyright Poetry Book Society and contributors. All rights reserved.
ISBN 9781913129095 ISSN 0551-1690

Supported using public funding by
ARTS COUNCIL ENGLAND

Poetry Book Society | Milburn House | Dean Street | Newcastle upon Tyne | NE1 1LF
0191 230 8100 | pbs@inpressbooks.co.uk

WWW.POETRYBOOKS.CO.UK

LETTER FROM THE PBS

"I want my poems to make you do the crying that leads to real thinking"
- Jericho Brown

The selected poets this season are truly international and the publications as a collection are wonderfully thought-provoking and full of impact. The poets lead us through ideas of race, identity, sexuality, fathers, alienation, and even the physics of spacetime. Our Charter members, who receive the PBS Choice and all four Recommendations, are in for a real treat! I really hope you enjoy this quarter's books and the selectors' commentaries as much as we have.

Do you write poetry as well as read it? We are delighted to announce that we have teamed up once again with Mslexia, to bring you the Women's Poetry and Pamphlet Prizes. Please do encourage any women you know to enter. You can follow our social media for regular writing inspiration and film interviews with poets including last year's prize winner, Penny Boxall. We look forward to reading your submissions.

We're also partnering with the Forward Prizes to offer book clubs across the country a huge discount on all ten shortlisted poetry books, ahead of the award ceremony at the Southbank Centre on the 20th of October. The Forward Prizes Book Club Bundle is only £60 (plus shipping) for PBS Members and includes invaluable reading notes, created by the Forward Prizes. If you run a book group or would like to set one up with other PBS members, email pbs@inpressbooks.co.uk for more information.

And finally, by popular demand, we now offer a recurring payment option, so your membership can automatically renew annually! Take a look at the enclosed order form or on our website to find out more and opt into auto renewals in the future.

SOPHIE O'NEILL
PBS & INPRESS DIRECTOR

Image: Stephanie Mitchell

JERICHO BROWN

Jericho Brown is the recipient of fellowships from the Guggenheim Foundation, the Radcliffe Institute for Advanced Study at Harvard, and the National Endowment for the Arts. Brown's first book, *Please* (New Issues, 2008), won the American Book Award. His second book, *The New Testament* (Copper Canyon, 2014), won the Anisfield-Wolf Book Award. His poems have appeared in *Buzzfeed*, *The New York Times*, *The New Yorker*, *TIME Magazine*, and several volumes of *The Best American Poetry*. He is an Associate Professor and Director of the Creative Writing Program at Emory University.

THE TRADITION

PICADOR | £10.99 | PBS PRICE £8.25

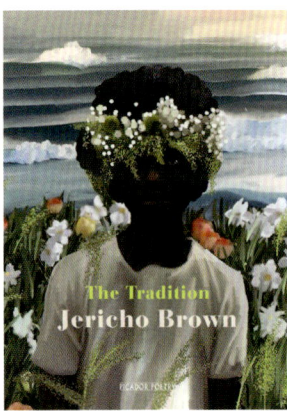

Jericho Brown is a veteran of lyrically graceful and emotionally powerful poetry. His latest collection, *The Tradition*, is no exception. Brown's work sometimes revolves around conceptions of the heroic and epic, taking mythology or its social patterns in order to interrogate whiteness and racial violence. In 'Hero' he writes "Black as a hero returning from war to a country that banked on his death. / Thank God. It can't get much darker than that." Operating between an impersonal plural and the specificities of the flesh, the poem exalts the lyric self to a kind of immortality, one of the preoccupations of a collection that concerns itself with death, divinity, the violent legacy of slavery and the vulnerabilities of the body.

In 'Riddle', a poem about the death of Emmett Till, an African-American teenager whose lynched and mutilated body in an open casket exposed American viewers to the brutality of racism, the poem's subject "we" is constructed out of a wilful aversion to responsibility. This collective subject cannot appropriate or make use of Till's mother's grief – it cannot be colonised, owned, or sold. This dilemma is laid bare by the lines:

> […] Shhh. We
> Can't take that sound. What is
> A mother wailing? We do not
> Recognize music until we can
> Sell it. We sell what cannot be
> Bought. We buy silence. Let us
> Help you. How much does it cost
> To hold your breath underwater?
> Wait. Wait. What are we? What?
> What on Earth are we? What?

The rhythms of Brown's work, its brevity a kind of incantation, allows for just this kind of inquiry to the reader. Very often there is hope and a celebratory imagining bound tightly with resistance and resilience. The book's third section links mortality (especially via HIV) and desire with a transcendent longing linked to faith but also sexuality. For Brown, the tradition running throughout these poems is a formal connection to black American writers. But it is also an unacknowledged lineage of embodiment, one that draws together the multiplicities of the self and offers readers a space to question their own becoming.

SANDEEP PARMAR

JERICHO BROWN

Here are some of the questions I find myself asking while writing poems: Do I love us enough? How is it that the same erotics that can lead to joy can also make way for violence? How narrow can the separation between tenderness and violence be? In a bed? In a family? What is a citizen in a nation that doesn't want my citizenship? What the hell is a man, and is he not built with the ability to listen?

I remain haunted by Plato's reasons for throwing poets out of the city. For him, the definition of a poet is the same as the definition for a person in love. The violent and apocalyptic world we have made for ourselves is also the world in which we fall in love. I believe art manages to stage in one place such contradictory aspects. My work, for instance, concerns itself with the ways love leads to touch and the fact that touch may well be an invasion. In my third book, *The Tradition*, I cut closer to the marrow with poems about my own experience with racial and sexual violation and about the way our nations have become invested in normalizing evil.

If your tears still mean anything to you, I want my poems to make you do the crying that leads to real thinking. And I want you to think yourself into the kind of action that old black people in the old black church called "conviction", as in, "And they which heard it, being convicted by their own conscience, went out one by one…" (John 8:9). Poems make it impossible to return to the world unbothered. I work to revise traditions.

JERICHO RECOMMENDS

Dustin Pearson's *Millennial Roost* (C & R Press) is never apologetic in its truth-telling or its disappointment at a world that goes on once awful truths are told. How do we live through (and live on!) after violation? While the horrors of this book challenge us, its voice is wry enough to enchant us. As much as these poems are anxious – "Make them describe it end to end" – they are also tender in their ability to dream –"I've been waiting for… closeness we wouldn't abuse."

BULLET POINTS

I will not shoot myself
In the head, and I will not shoot myself
In the back, and I will not hang myself
With a trashbag, and if I do,
I promise you, I will not do it
In a police car while handcuffed
Or in the jail cell of a town
I only know the name of
Because I have to drive through it
To get home. Yes, I may be at risk,
But I promise you, I trust the maggots
Who live beneath the floorboards
Of my house to do what they must
To any carcass more than I trust
An officer of the law of the land
To shut my eyes like a man
Of God might, or to cover me with a sheet
So clean my mother could have used it
To tuck me in. When I kill me, I will
Do it the same way most Americans do,
I promise you: cigarette smoke
Or a piece of meat on which I choke
Or so broke I freeze
In one of these winters we keep
Calling worst. I promise if you hear
Of me dead anywhere near
A cop, then that cop killed me. He took
Me from us and left my body, which is,
No matter what we've been taught,
Greater than the settlement
A city can pay a mother to stop crying,
And more beautiful than the new bullet
Fished from the folds of my brain.

THE TRADITION

Aster. Nasturtium. Delphinium. We thought
Fingers in dirt meant it was our dirt, learning
Names in heat, in elements classical
Philosophers said could change us. *Stargazer.*
Foxglove. Summer seemed to bloom against the will
Of the sun, which news reports claimed flamed hotter
On this planet than when our dead fathers
Wiped sweat from their necks. *Cosmos. Baby's Breath.*
Men like me and my brothers filmed what we
Planted for proof we existed before
Too late, sped the video to see blossoms
Brought in seconds, colors you expect in poems
Where the world ends, everything cut down.
John Crawford. Eric Garner. Mike Brown.

Image: Julian Knox

ANTHONY ANAXAGOROU

Anthony Anaxagorou is a British Cypriot award-winning poet, fiction writer, essayist, curator and publisher. He has written several volumes of poetry, a spoken-word EP and a collection of short stories. He's an honorary fellow at the University of Roehampton where he lectures in the social sciences. His poetry has appeared in *Poetry*, *The Poetry Review*, *Poetry London*, *Granta*, *The Rialto*, *Oxford Poetry*, *Wildness*, *The Feminist Review* and elsewhere. It's also been featured on BBC Radio 4, BBC Newsnight, BBC Radio London, ITV, Vice UK, Channel 4 and Sky Arts.

AFTER THE FORMALITIES
PENNED IN THE MARGINS | £9.99 | PBS PRICE £7.50

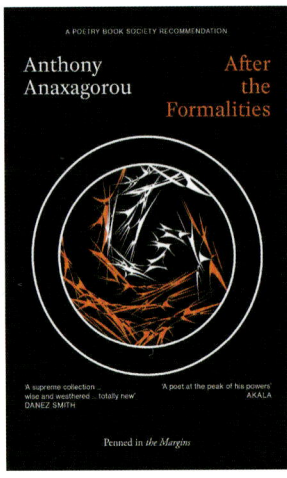

Anthony Anaxagorou's *After the Formalities* might reverse William Carlos Williams' oft-quoted line from *Paterson*: "no ideas but in things". Things do, of course, abound throughout Anaxagorou's poems, but it is the idea that drives many of them discursively into an interrogation of how forms of language and meaning are historicised. Words become archival materials, reticent of singularity, making the self also multiple in their layering as they pass through human hands and the poet's imagination. The collection's title poem illustrates this by combining reflections on migration and otherness with the origins of the word, and categorisation of, "race". Quotations punctuate more lyric material, drawing on hundreds of years of usage and pointing unequivocally to Brexit and its contemporary contexts. From Jacques de Brézé's poem 'The Hunt', which first coins "race" in 1481 in relation to dogs, to Charles Darwin, Winston Churchill, Enoch Powell and Nigel Farage, among others, Anaxagorou implicitly likens the violence of taxonomies to narratives of empire (the British in Cyprus and beyond), nostalgia, loss and masculinity.

> After the formalities of course I said London
> and of course he asked again. When I said Cyprus
> he leaned into his chair recalling a family holiday.
> The weather sublime. The people accommodating.
> Particularly towards the English. How it was a shame
> about the Turkish thing. And your parents. When did they enter
> here? In the late '50s I replied. So before the Immigrants Act?
> Yes I said. Before. Well good for them. He said.
> Putting the lid on his pen. Closing his pad.

The formalities here are both the poetic form, assuming a literary space for self-determination that is neutral, and the formal mode of address that requires pinning the body to a space of designation. These spaces lie uneasily together as relational in the philosophical equivocations of speech. Elsewhere, in 'Nautical Almanac', the speaker's engagement with fatherhood is tender and searching, laying the groundwork for unanswered histories to be resolved in another life. Driven by an energetic thinking and intellect, these poems navigate across an aesthetic and conceptual domain with constant and impressive sureness.

SANDEEP PARMAR

ANTHONY ANAXAGOROU

In *After the Formalities* I was considering the role biography can play in assisting with the way we think not only about the construct of race, fatherhood and masculinity, but the interconnectedness of our lives which overlaps and contradicts itself. I've always felt my own ethnicity as a Cypriot has meant I exist at a strange intersection where several key social signifiers collide. It's around this area where I focused much of the writing, particularly the poems concerned with race science and feelings of otherness, or in what Nuar Alsadir calls in *Fourth Person Singular* "the elsewhere... the embodied self with concurrent selves in alternate space-times".

Today's social groups are incredibly complex and mercurial, so I wanted to calibrate a poetic which had the facility to reach into those precarious fissures, and probe using history and real-life events, moving the reader deeper into those spaces. To create poetry without the need for constant revelation, but instead to draw upon some of the more nuanced anxieties and confusions borne out of the ways we perceive each other, became a hugely liberating part of the book's two-year development.

There are poems where I wanted to implicate the reader, a decision I agonised over, then there are poems which hopefully propose relief in some capacity, or delight, or restoration, or perhaps even a bleakness. The poems about my relationship with my father felt at times unkind and exposing yet, being a new father myself, I wanted that tension to contrast my childhood with my personal and direct experiences of fatherhood. In such hostile times this collection is very much focused on plurality, where the "I" refused to sit still, the poetic risks involved were high, and the arguments extensive.

ANTHONY RECOMMENDS

Matthew Sweeney, *My Life As A Painter* (Bloodaxe); Morgan Parker, *Magical Negro* (Tin House), Rebecca Goss, *Girl* (Carcanet); Natalie Scenters-Zapico, *Lima :: Limón* (Copper Canyon Press); Mona Arshi, *Dear Big Gods* (Pavilion); Jenny Xie, *Eye Level* (Graywolf); Jen Campbell, *The Girl Aquarium* (Bloodaxe); Rachael Allen, *Kingdomland* (Faber); Ada Limón, *Bright Dead Things* (Milkweed); Jay Bernard, *Surge* (Chatto); Rebecca Tamás, *WITCH* (Penned in the Margins); Kim Hyesoon, *Autobiography of Death* (New Directions); Gboyega Odubanjo, *While I Yet Live* (Bad Betty Press); Kim Kyung Ju, translated by Jake Levine, *Crying For No Reason* (clinic) and Ilya Kaminsky, *Deaf Republic* (Faber).

you will ask

                wanting the tunnel to explain
                its darkness

needing the answer
to be more than echo

Image: Zigmunds Lapsa

SYMPATHY FOR RAIN

Only a flood will be keen to want more
cities run you into their concrete cage
umbrellas fatten to confirm your   waste
roof tiles keep you only for your slickness
spectacles bury you   in a tissue's
neat secret   leather jokes at your attempt
little refugees of somewhere cloud   camped
in stained-glass windows what thug-grey did this
even when you soak through cloth to beg skin
you're shaken off   left to dry into loss
a slant of earth still motions your   saving
a slug slow as a monk carries you   up
asking red to soften around your name
until you are nowhere   but there   again.

MARY JEAN CHAN

Mary Jean Chan is a poet, editor and critic from Hong Kong. Her debut pamphlet *A Hurry of English* was selected as the 2018 Poetry Book Society Summer Pamphlet Choice. In 2017, she was shortlisted for the Forward Prize for Best Single Poem, and is currently shortlisted for the 2019 Forward Prizes in the same category. An editor of *Oxford Poetry*, advisory board member at the Poetry Translation Centre and member of the Folio Prize Academy, Mary Jean is a Lecturer in Creative Writing (Poetry) at Oxford Brookes University and lives in London. *Flèche* (Faber & Faber) is her first full collection.

FLÈCHE

FABER | £10.99 | PBS PRICE £8.25

Mary Jean Chan's debut collection, *Flèche*, is prefaced by five statements that one expects to speak to the book's central concerns. I would suggest this is partly true; Chan's writing does grapple with self definition; the preconceptions a reader might bring about the author's identity; monolingualism, as a way of instituting silence and control, and love. But by raising these so prominently, Chan also makes her reader aware of the contradictions within these ideas. Is this "a book of love poems"? By which the poet means, perhaps, what is a book of love poems? To whom does English belong, if it is spoken by one who wrestles with colonial narration about the other, but for whom it is also a means of self definition? Here we find poems that approach familial relations, desire, as well as political and social borders of the self. The brilliant and complex ways in which Chan inhabits the rightly enigmatic or aphoristic space raised by the (often revelatory) preface are multiple, vibrant, compelling.

The collection's title poem refers directly to a skilful lunge manoeuvre in fencing, itself a term that derives from the French word for "arrow". The stride, the vector, the shaping of a female queer subject position engage with matters of the flesh, an intended echo.

Parry riposte

My greatest weakness: the *riposte*. In the changing room, the girl I was about to duel said I smelled of bitter gourd. We were practicing the *flèche*. Inevitably, I collided with her, a blur of entangled blades. I glimpsed her wry expression through our masks' steel mesh: her gleaming, smiling lips.

Chan's language, even here in a prose lyric form, is strategic and sharp, a kind of heightened articulation that handles each word as a possible weapon. Elsewhere we see the same precision that deploys object, image and syntax with every knowledge of the page as a *piste* (in fencing terms, the area of play) for discovery. In 'Splitting' she writes:

> the poet does not understand everything
> but being self-award knows enough to say
> *splitting is a defence* *mechanism* against
> love and its absences

SANDEEP PARMAR

MARY JEAN CHAN

Flèche denotes an offensive, aggressive fencing technique that is favoured by épéeists. As a former competitive fencer who represented my home city, Hong Kong, at international tournaments, I wanted to use this cross-linguistic pun to evoke the queer, racialised body as both vulnerable "flesh" and weaponised "flèche". Furthermore, the art of duelling productively embodies instances of conflict which I have experienced in response to homophobia and its legacies of queer shame. Through dividing the book into three main sections ('Parry', 'Riposte' and 'Corps-à-Corps'), I seek to trace my personal and poetic journey from an emotionally defensive position towards a willingness to engage in metaphorical combat. In doing so, I explore in my work intersectional identities including gender, sexuality and race, as well as related themes of queerness, postcolonialism and multilingualism.

I write a lot about mothers: generations of women who have lived through political turmoil in 20th century China. My poem 'Wet Nurse' seeks to remember the woman who raised my mother, but who made the painfully complex decision to abandon her own daughter in order to find work in Shanghai as a wet nurse. Poems about my mother's childhood mingle memory and myth; after decades of retelling, her stories are ones which I have since sought to transform through the lens of my experiences of growing up with intergenerational trauma. I also wish to honour the power and complexity of familial relationships: "We drink in a serene / silence, my mother smiles a smile / that breaks my breath into laughter" ('Tea Ceremony'). The lover is also a central figure in this collection. In 'They Would Have All That', I write: "They are gentler because they have / grown too knowledgeable to love any other way." This is a book of love poems, and ultimately, a work of hope.

MARY JEAN RECOMMENDS

Rachael Allen, *Kingdomland* (Faber); Raymond Antrobus, *The Perseverance* (Penned in the Margins); Mona Arshi, *Dear Big Gods* (Pavilion); Fiona Benson, *Vertigo & Ghost* (Cape); Jay Bernard, *Surge* (Chatto); Chen Chen, *When I Grow Up I Want to be a List of Further Possibilities* (Bloodaxe); Will Harris, *RENDANG* (Granta); Ilya Kaminsky, *Deaf Republic* (Faber); Sandeep Parmar, Nisha Ramayya and Bhanu Kapil, *Threads* (clinic); Rebecca Tamás, *WITCH* (Penned in the Margins); Layli Long Soldier, *Whereas* (Picador) and Jane Yeh, *Discipline* (Carcanet).

The way skin   is never an apology

Image: Cody T. Davis

NOTES TOWARDS AN UNDERSTANDING

I.

When you said: *Why didn't you warn me about cultural differences?* I did not know whether you meant my mother's face all darkened like a curtain, or the vegetables.

II.

When mother said: *The contours of her ears are calamitous*, I momentarily reflected on my own auditory shells, whether they too played a part in my irrevocable queerness.

III.

When father said: *I find language to be a very difficult thing*, I wondered if he was apologising for his silences, how he said nothing when mother detonated my name.

IV.

When I said: *I want to shout at all of you, but in which language?* My mind was tuned to two frequencies: mother's Cantonese rage, your soothing English, inviting me to choose.

Image: Billie Riley

SENI SENEVIRATNE

Seni Seneviratne, born and raised in Leeds, is of English and Sri Lankan heritage. She has published two previous poetry collections *Wild Cinnamon and Winter Skin* (2007) and *The Heart of It* (2012) with Peepal Tree Press. Her poem 'Operation Cast Lead' was shortlisted in the Arvon International Poetry Competition (2010). She is a fellow of the Complete Works programme for diversity and quality in British Poetry and has collaborated with film-makers, visual artists, musicians and digital artists. She is currently one of ten commissioned writers on the *Colonial Countryside Project: National Trust Houses Reinterpreted*. She lives in Derbyshire and works as a freelance writer.

UNKNOWN SOLDIER
PEEPAL TREE PRESS | £9.99 | PBS PRICE £7.50

The poet's father was the one brown (Sri Lankan) face in his army platoon. He speaks in this book, as does "Shorty", his mate and sometime photographer:

He's got the sun behind him, but the light's too bright.
It'll be a bugger to develop, with Snowball's dark skin

against the pale tent canvas. We're not framed right.

The rhyme – an alternative sort of (poetic) framing – denatures the voice, without killing its intimacy. Our memories blur into photographs: children internalise the pictures they're shown, or it's the self-conscious experience of posing or being posed for the lens that's mentally rehearsed, reinforced and repeated. It's North Africa, 1941 – full of misunderstandings and homosocial abrasiveness:

...Corporal gets back from leave
in Cairo telling us he's been to a "wog-barber".
Then it's all eyes on me. Waiting for a reaction.

"Snowball" is an ironic nickname, like Robin Hood's Little John – "I noticed Snowball first on the troopship. / He was different to the other lads"– central to a politically incorrect tendresse, which echoes our ache, in safety and peacetime, to reach across equivalent boundaries: "I imagined striking up a conversation with him / but couldn't figure out how". Seneviratne's forms provide the point of entry into the personae (for both poet and reader), while acknowledging (those rhymes, those stanzas) the distance imaginatively crossed. Which two soldiers try to laugh off:

Since he doesn't look English and he's a chap
you can be straight with, I just blurt out,

"How come you landed up so far away from
where you were born?" Then I see his face.
Before or since, I've never seen the like of this.

This poem's called 'Talking About Home' – a word which doesn't mean the same thing to both men – and the slant-rhyme on "face" and "this" is wonderfully affecting. The words belong together, but not quite. They resemble each other, they converse, but they aren't the same. Or are they?

VIDYAN RAVINTHIRAN

SENI SENEVIRATNE

This collection, born out of silences, became an elegy for my late father and a monument to things that were unspoken between us. At its heart is an album of black and white photographs taken by an unknown photographer. It is the only surviving record of a friendship between two signalmen who met for the first time in May 1941 in an army camp in the North African desert. The subject of the photographs is my father, a young man from Ceylon, serving as a radio operator in the Royal Corps of Signals. Like so many who came back, "He never spoke much more about the War".

He died in 1988 before he was old enough for nostalgia and before I was ready to ask the questions. I lived with the photographs and the regret, for some years, before I began to look for the voices of the two men and the story behind the images. They meet again at the beginning of this book with "a conversation about moors and poetry and the language of photos."

Once I found their voices, it created the space for me to meet my father, the *Unknown Soldier*, to write what I don't know, to have the conversations I had longed for and to grieve for his losses and mine:

> Does this seem odd? This replying to letters
> sent, all those years ago, from a troopship?
>
> What with me not due to be born for another
> ten years and you dead now this past thirty.
>
> No matter. I know you, at least, believed in
> an afterlife so I'll hope you are receiving me.

These poems were written in the quiet of an early morning bird hide where the themes of migration and survival are ever present, resonating with my father's story as well as recent tragedies of migrant deaths in the face of Fortress Europe.

SENI RECOMMENDS

I keep going back to Mimi Khalvati's *The Weather Wheel*, and I'm looking forward to her next book, *Afterwardness* (Carcanet). I highly recommend two debut pamphlets published this year: Chloe Balcomb's *Waney Edge* (Green Bottle Press) and Seán Hewitt's *Lantern* (Offord Road Books). Maria Jastrzebska *The True Story of Cowboy Hat and Ingenue* (Cinnamon Press), Natalie Diaz's *When My Brother was an Aztec* (Copper Canyon Press), Zeina Hashem Beck's *Louder than Hearts* (Bauhan Publishing), Raymond Antrobus' *The Perseverance* (Penned in the Margins). And always Audre Lorde.

Can I capture it in black and white?

Image of Seni Seneviratne's father "Snowball"

NEVER A WORD

I'm trying to decipher the paperwork from the MOD,
or match the thumbprint in his soldiers service book,

and the story sways away from me – the way he'd sway
with my mum at those dinner dances, in his leather-soled

dancing shoes. He tried to teach me the steps of a waltz
or a foxtrot. Me with my mod haircut, long down one side

over my eyes and two corkscrew curls by my ears.
This digging is exhausting and never a word from him.

What about his memories that went underground and
stay there with the weight of his headstone on them?

Image: Enda Wyley

PETER SIRR

The Gravity Wave is Peter Sirr's tenth collection of poems with The Gallery Press. Other recent titles include *Sway* (2016), versions of poems from the troubadour tradition; *The Rooms* (2014), shortlisted for the *Irish Times* Poetry Now Award and the Pigott Poetry Prize and *The Thing Is* (2009), awarded the Michael Hartnett Prize. A novel for children, *Black Wreath*, was published in 2014 and RTE has broadcast several radio plays. A regular critic and essayist, he lives in Dublin with his wife, the poet Enda Wyley, and daughter. He is a member of Aosdána, an affiliation of creative artists in Ireland.

THE GRAVITY WAVE
THE GALLERY PRESS | £10.50 | PBS PRICE £7.88

Peter Sirr draws on the classics – Homer, Catullus, Sappho; and, moving on, Borges, Kafka, Brueghel – to ask if we, in comparison, live in a disenchanted (cynical, money-straitened) world:

> Diminished? Really? Gods don't hold us, the temples wither, the priests are all in sales
> but the sun still shines, the oxen low
> and the winedark sea is still as dark as wine.

He acknowledges world-traumas – the Final Solution, "Shahad, Rawan, Maram / this hand in the rubble / these broken shutters / shrapnel on the bed cover"– while risking, as Auden had it, a voice of affirmation and praise:

> We're in there, obsolescing, the tapes frayed.
> We might be Hittites. And yet
> let the technologies rot. The air holds us
> and no one comes to see it, no one
> interrogates it...

I admire this book for how it registers the weight of the world, and also for its creative resistance – milder than impassioned, stronger than incidental – to the brutality of the actual. Sirr combines vivid forms, their hewn heft (recalling Derek Mahon) with a felicitously wrongfooting weirdness, all of his own: "as if here we might be, when it's all over, / walking through fields of Lidl"; "the deviceless avenue / notified by trees, alerted / by fuchsia, montbretia".

These poems rediscover value – "the water brought from the stream / the hay made / while the sun loiters on the desk" – in the frailest locales: "earth unstepped on, air / unpushed through, where / smallness abounds, dust // feasts...". Each poem seems written with immense care, not only to arrange words scintillatingly, but also to preserve the briefest, most otherwise-ephemeral details. Reading these poems, we're reminded that exactly where we're vulnerable is where change is possible:

> There's a room inside us we've never settled,
> never owned.
> To get there is to find the movers
> have just filled their van
> and driven off.

VIDYAN RAVINTHIRAN

PETER SIRR

The Gravity Wave is bookended by poems about time. The title poem reflects my obsession with this image from physics: a gravity or gravitational wave is a disturbance in the fabric of spacetime, maybe a great cosmic event like black holes merging, but by the time we receive the ripple's signal it's infinitesimally smaller, measured by very sensitive instruments. I wanted to think of that in human terms, of gestures, emotions, the fabric of a life somehow continuing to ramify, to "pour down the billennia" even when the original human impulses are dark stars.

Maybe it's because I live in the centre of an old city, with its constant irruption of past into present and the looming crane-heavy future staking its claim, that I have this sense of layers, of having a foot in several time zones simultaneously. The book opens with a series of sonnets that plays with that notion. I'd been reading *The Odyssey* a lot and it kept creeping into everything I was writing. 'The Now Slice' mixes up a floundering Odysseus, my daughter starting secondary school and the idea that a creature ten billion light years away can experience the same "now" as we do, inhabits the same "now slice" as the scientists have it. And this all gets mixed up with mortality, memory, ghost poems and elegies.

Music is everywhere – a riff on Schubert, poems that respond to Max Richter responding to Kafka or a performance of Monteverdi's *Return of Ulysses*. Place, as always, figures heavily, the streets of Dublin, the mountains and sea of Kerry, our quick, nervy passage through it all. But these are the incidentals; the poet's relationship with poetry is always a bit slant. Whatever the ostensible subject, what you're really looking for is some kind psychic acceleration – Brodsky's "accelerated thinking" – that bears you out of yourself. I love that Miroslav Holub definition: "Poetry is energy, it is an energy-storing and energy-releasing device." You're always looking to get at that energy, to let the poem that's buried deep inside you come out and blaze if it can.

PETER RECOMMENDS

Antonella Anedda, *Archipelago*, trans. Jamie McKendrick (Bloodaxe); Yves Bonnefoy, *Poems*, eds. Anthony Rudolf, John Naughton and Stephen Romer (Carcanet); Denise Riley, *Say Something Back* (Picador); Czeslaw Milosz (ed.), *A Book of Luminous Things: An International Anthology of Poetry*; Seán Ó Coileáin, *Seán Ó Ríordáin: Life and Work*, translated by Mícheál Ó hAodha, (Mercier Press); Tony Hoagland, *Real Sofisticashun: Essays on poetry and craft* (Graywolf Press); Chris Torrance, *The Magic Door* (Test Centre); Peter Huchel, *Garden of Theophrastus: Selected Poems* (Anvil); Tom Pickard, *Winter Migrants* (Carcanet); Alastair Reid, *Barefoot: The Collected Poems*, ed. Tom Pow (Galileo); Helen Dunmore, *Counting Backwards: Poems 1975-2017* (Bloodaxe).

Let the room be lit by her
and listen

Image: 'Indigo Moon Series IV' by Kate MacDonagh

THE GRAVITY WAVE

Where next for this gust
printing itself on your dress,
catching the rim of your hat, riffing
in the strands of your hair?

Maybe the same place
as this single breath, this turning
of neck towards neck,
this widening of the eyes and whatever

loosens behind,
soul-stretch, spirit-drift
that have left us and gone
pouring down the billennia,

rippling, thinning,
fainter by the second but lodged forever,
infinitesimally measurable
where two particles conversing

almost falter, almost alter
as they register
the micron's micron, the hair's breadth's whisper
of what passed between us.

Image: Alisa Tricoli-Bugan

CARMEN BUGAN

Carmen Bugan was born in Romania in 1970 and emigrated to the US with her family in 1989. She has a doctorate in English Literature from Balliol College, Oxford. Her previous publications include three collections of poems, a critical study on *Seamus Heaney and East European Poetry in Translation: Poetics of Exile*, and the internationally acclaimed memoir *Burying the Typewriter: Childhood Under the Eye of the Secret Police* (Picador). A recipient of an Arts Council grant, Bugan was a Creative Arts Fellow in Literature at Wolfson College, Oxford University, and is a Fellow of the George Orwell Prize. In 2018 she was the Helen DeRoy Professor in Honors at the University of Michigan specialising in Poetry and the Language of Oppression.

LILIES FROM AMERICA: NEW & SELECTED

SHEARSMAN | £10.95 | PBS PRICE £8.22

Carmen Bugan was born in Romania, and writes of imprisonment and harassment; the crimes of the Securitate; the manifold deprivations, and the culture of surveillance, prior to the Revolution. Personal and political events mingle their time-signatures: "Hours swelled / Like the shadows of passing black trucks / Loaded with criminals". What survives of this, as a salve and a guarantee of futurity, are trees, flowers, and the rituals which once made sense of people's lives and deaths, as in this poem for the writer's grandmother:

> The mourners put their hands together
> Under the black ribbons above the doors,
> And sing of her eyebrows turning into moss
> Her eyes turning into violets,
> Her bones turning into flutes.

Bugan writes with glittering precision: "Bursts of sun dust / Thousands of yellow and violet flowers". Her syntax elegantly reassesses the memories of exile: "All things I wanted to forget / Crowd in-between the lines I spent years writing: / Four languages, ambitions, homesickness, dispersed friends". There are things you want to forget, and things to remember; but memory is no secure possession.

> To her it was a row of whitewashed houses
> Rising from the sea; she said the whiteness
> Appears and vanishes behind crests of waves.
>
> A wooden gate with a blue rope latch
> Was mine; and the path between
> Pear and quince.

Bugan always finds the right word, yet her poems accept how little this act – in the real-world sense – accomplishes. 'Visiting the country of my birth' begins with the execution of the Ceaușescus, before suggesting, with a deeply heartening persuasiveness, that the past can be recovered just when hope is given up: "Unblemished sky ripples inside the tin bucket, / Cradled in my arms the way I used to hold / Warm goose eggs close to skin so not to break them".

SELECTOR'S COMMENT

VIDYAN RAVINTHIRAN

CROSSING THE CARPATHIANS WITH YOU

for my mother

Mountains and us clothed
In soft white fog,
Suddenness of cliffs.

You and I carve walking sticks,
Bursts of sun dust
Thousands of yellow and violet flowers.

Red and white polka-dot
Mushrooms among trees,
Strong smell of ferns and cones.

Stones in pots on our backs
Warnings to black bears,
We gather forget-me-nots.

Distant curves
Of snow and peaks
In the white of the moon.

Shepherds' rain fast and thin
We empty the boots of water,
A bear licks out pots.

I know what it means to go
Anywhere with you: you are
The moss on which I sleep.

Image Tony Ward

MANUEL FORCANO

Manuel Forcano was born in 1968 in Barcelona and has a PhD in Semitic Philology. He completed his studies in Israel, Syria and Egypt and has worked as a Lecturer in Hebrew and Aramaic at the University of Barcelona (1996-2004). He has translated literary works from Hebrew, Arabic, French, English and Italian, published anthologies of his own poems including *Corint* (winner of the Barcelona Jocs Florals Prize, 2000), *The Baghdad Train*, winner of the Carles Riba Prize, 2003, and *Law Governing Aliens*, which was awarded the Qwerty Prize, 2008.

Anna Crowe studied French and Spanish at the University of St Andrews where she now lives, working as a writer and translator. She has also been a primary school teacher and worked for many years in the Quarto second-hand bookshop. She has tutored for the Arvon Foundation, and led poetry workshops for almost twenty years.

MAPS OF DESIRE
MANUEL FORCANO TRANSLATED BY ANNA CROWE
ARC PUBLICATIONS | £11.99 | PBS PRICE £8.25

Perhaps the strangest of the translation submissions this time, but definitely delightful, is the translation of a seventeenth century Latin poem, *Coffee*, by the French poet Guillaume Massieu, rendered, rather wonderfully into archaic rhyming couplets by John T Gilmore. As the title indicates, the poem is about coffee as much as the eighteenth century English poet, John Phillips' *Cyder* is about cider. The discursive-descriptive poem-essay was a staple of the eighteenth century. If there were a prize for such things I wouldn't hesitate to give it to the translation of *Coffee*.

But there isn't in this case, so my choice is Manuel Forcano's *Maps of Desire*. Forcano deals with gay desire with a whirlwind-like freshness and a passionate imagination that does at times remind me a little of Cavafy with a gale behind him, some of the poems being written in Cavafy's own city, Alexandria. Forcano is a many-sided scholar but he is primarily an outstanding lyric poet, beautifully rendered into English by Anna Crowe. The book begins with two sections of 'The Baghdad Train', a sweeping journey in pursuit of desire. Here is a fragment from "Checkmate":

> …I got drunk just seeing you,
> and playing chess was an excuse
> for watching your fingers
> moving the pieces of your army
> towards me. How sweet
> it can sometimes turn out to be,
> being defeated: on the board
> your castle knocking over
> my king.
> Many nights
> you lined up your pawns
> to face me.

This leaves all too little space to praise Agnes Scott Langeland's translations of the Norwegian Stein Mehren's *To the Outermost Stars* which is also excellent and the Iranian Modernist Bijan Elahi's fine *High Tide of the Eyes* published by The Operating System. Both deserve buying and reading. Buy them all.

SELECTOR'S COMMENT

GEORGE SZIRTES

THE BAGHDAD TRAIN

For some time you've been travelling underground
passing through the dark tunnel of your desire,
and the gentle jolting of the metro
brings you, brings to that winter body of yours,
the summer and the heat of loose clothing
of that journey on the Baghdad train
that pulled out late and full to bursting
from Aleppo's Central Station,
Syria. Third class:
carriages without doors,
windows without glass, iron seats,
country people, soldiers, djellabas and turbans,
dishevelled garments, golden tan on necks,
arms, hands, voices, bare
feet, each one a son of Apollo,
you'd say. A great piling-up,
heat and more heat, very little room:
hours of travel deciding whether or not to lick
an unmoving drop of sweat
so close to you that you are a tree
rooted in that, the only water.
In the toilets of the damaged carriages
sex between the rust and the cracked mirror.
The wheels were snatching sighs
from the rails. "Because I've come
to fasten you to myself in thirst,"
he told you, when your mouths parted.
Love is also a kind of speed:
with a caress, a landscape
that is a monotone of nothingness bursts
suddenly into the green of orchards with water tanks,
and from the topmost blossom on the palm tree
you see how the white ibis takes off.

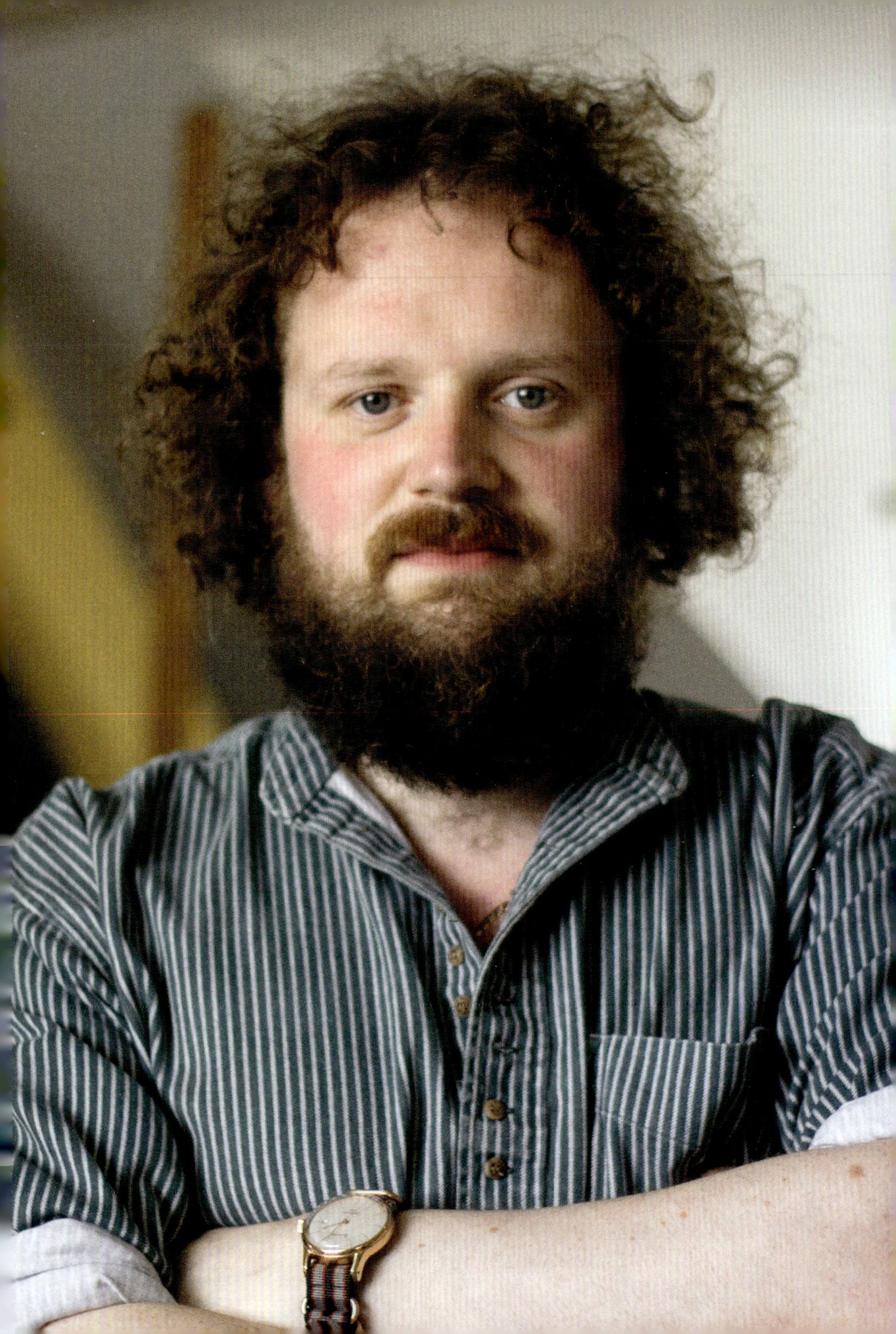

SCOTT McKENDRY

Scott McKendry is currently studying towards a Ph.D. in poetry at Queen's University Belfast. His poems have appeared in *The future always makes me so thirsty: New Poets from the North of Ireland* (Blackstaff, 2016), *The North, Tangerine, Public Illumination* Magazine, *The Manchester Review, Magma, Cyphers* and *Poetry Ireland Review*.

CURFUFFLE

SCOTT McKENDRY | THE LIFEBOAT | £6.50

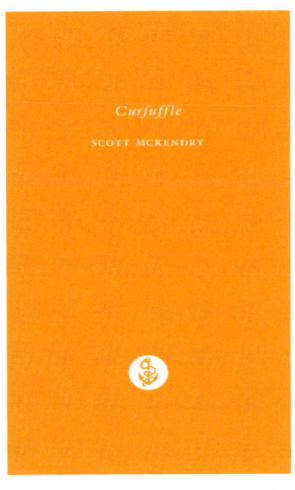

Scott McKendry is not overly concerned with the introversions of the Lyric Tradition: "Bradypus variegates, the brown-throated three-toed sloth, / is surely the laziest bastard in the South American jungle." His style is instantly recognisable: the male Northern Irish line of Paul Muldoon, Ciaran Carson, Alan Gillis, with its love for ludic extravagance, the shaggy dog story, the conversationally convoluted. Like Gillis, he finds joy in the vocabulary of the local: "true bill", "swoll", "gub", "jouked", "deadon", "ganch", which, along with a passion for sensory detail and contemporary trivia, gives him the additional Scottish air of Roddy Lumsden.

Also like Gillis, the violence and socio-political particularities of Northern Ireland are bent through a prism of drink, drugs, and dreams; there is a common turn towards the phantasmagoric, the trippy. In 'Zawba'ah, Lord of Friday, the Planet Venus, the Colour Green and Iron', Hermetic magic meets Captain Beefheart meets marijuana:

> ...I crooned,
> *Abba Zaba go-zoom. Babbette baboon – Babbette baboon.*

In 'Male Line: A Fallacy', McKendry plays on the absurdity of patriarchal verities and cultural polarities:

> My grandfather was a hippy, man, he dropped LSD
> at Woodstock; his father went to war at seventeen
> after the Zimmerman telegram, and *his* daddy
> was an original Klansman from Pulaski, Tennessee,
> whose daddio, an Orangeman, marched from Bangor
> to Donaghadee, funny that, because his father's father
> was a United Irishman, whose grandpa, a butcher's boy,
> held the gate at Derry...

Masonic ritual meets The Flintstones in 'Keepers of the Pedigree', an iconoclastic squib in the vein of Ian Duhig; in other poems, with unquestioning regularity, households are invaded by real characters presenting real threats. McKendry writes in the dizzy zone between injurious downfall and comedic uproar. It's worth bending your ear to it.

A.B. JACKSON & DEGNA STONE

WHO SEPARATES US

for Matthew Rice and his da; after Adrian Rice and his Matthew

It wasn't so much that we burnt tyres, releasing a toxic stew
    of nasties,
or that each Eleventh Night, as a spat crescendoed, some fella
    got battered
or worse, wound up dead, after an adversary went in hard
    with a nine iron;
or the dearth of historical fervour, despite our fertile preteen
    minds,
orgulous for no reason but our labours, and addled with
    WKD
Orange, which – sickly-sweet – was then the only flavour;
or the hazard of a gaunt older boy who could barely hold the
    AKM
or, as it recoiled, keep its spray above the throng, after twelve
    MGD

or Bud. It was that they burnt our hut – our casern for to
    watch the pile
(or that's what we told our mas), in which we drank and
    joked and made out,
or made out we had, into teenhood – a lodge of pallets
    roofed with bitumen felt
or ancient paisley carpet, decked out with filthy sofas and a
    kerosene lamp
or a million-candle torch commandeered from some
    neighbour's shed.
Every tenth of July, in the morning, the Coalman turned up
    with a jerrican.

Image: Nina Subin

DUNYA MIKHAIL

Dunya Mikhail was born in Baghdad, Iraq, and moved to the United States thirty years later in 1995. After graduating from the University of Baghdad, she worked as a journalist and translator for the *Baghdad Observer*. Facing censorship and interrogation, she left Iraq, first to Jordan and then to America, settling in Detroit. Her books include *The Beekeeper of Sinjar*, *The Iraqi Nights*, *Diary of A Wave Outside the Sea* and *The War Works Hard*. She is also the editor of *15 Iraqi Poets* and has received a Guggenheim Fellowship, a Knights Foundation grant, a Kresge Fellowship and the United Nations Human Rights Award for Freedom of Writing. Mikhail works as a Lecturer of Arabic at Oakland University in Michigan.

IN HER FEMININE SIGN

CARCANET | £12.99 | PBS PRICE £8.25

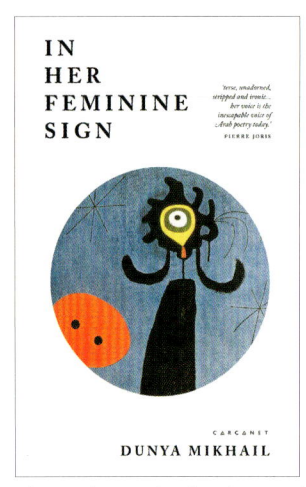

Dunya Mikhail's *In Her Feminine Sign* is very much a collection of poems which follow the Iraqi-born poet through a set of interconnected thoughts revolving around language, home and gender. In the opening author's note Mikhail remarks how "I wrote these poems from right to left and from left to right. I didn't translate them, I only wrote them twice." The Arabic version is not present in the book, which again can be interpreted as its own inverted statement. To be told two languages are at play, but to be presented with only one, could be seen as the markings of displacement, the compromise of involuntary exile. There is also a deep and constant drive towards an idea of home or belonging that occurs throughout the book. In the poem 'The Gypsy' we're told, "She doesn't care much about transformations between day and night although she's puzzled and amazed by the moon, how it passes her by like a train disappearing with its passengers until it stops at the last station, finally alone."

The collection, broken in three sections 'The Tied Circle', 'Tablets' and 'T/here' calls upon various dualities to reckon with wider ideas of home, identity and America's relationship to the Middle East. "To capture the poem in two lives is to mirror my exile, with all its possibilities and risks." Mikhail fled to the US in the mid-90s after being put on Saddam Hussein's enemies list. The section titled 'Tablets' consists of a litany of numbered poems which aphoristically work to push us into questioning the positions and spaces we occupy, "The butterfly that flew a moment ago over the killed ones was the soul searching for home." Notions of war, alienation and longing are ubiquitous, yet it's the desire to call a place of origin "home" that keeps finding its way back into the lines,"The spider makes a home outside itself. It doesn't call it exile."

In Her Feminine Sign is a wise and innovative set of poems which ask us to consider not only what it means to be living away from home, but how home can shift depending on a number of variables. How welcomed a person might feel in their new country is something beyond their control, and Mikhail captures those anxieties and paradoxes perfectly: "The Earth is so simple, you can explain it with a tear or a laugh. The Earth is so complicated, you need a tear or a laugh to explain it."

ANTHONY ANAXAGOROU

DUNYA MIKHAIL

Arabic language is gender-oriented. Everything is either a "he" or a "she", no "it." The feminine words are distinguished with a symbol called *taa-marbuta* (a circle with two dots above it that's inserted as a suffix.) The literal meaning of "marbuta" is "tied." The tied circle obsessed me, more than any time before, in August 2014 when a market was opened to buy and sell women in Iraq and Syria and elsewhere online. The market was called "*suq al-sabaya*" (female slaves market) opened by Daesh (ISIS) members who considered women as property. They "tied" their hands and dragged them into the unknown. I had the chance to speak with some of those women who escaped and made it back home. In addition to documenting their pain in the non-fiction book, *The Beekeeper of Sinjar*, I reacted with poems that are included in this collection.

Another section of the book consists of Iraqi Haiku which unfold like Sumerian symbols carved onto clay tablets, transmuted into the stuff of our daily life and into the digital tablets we carry with us to Mars. This book is the first one that I've written in both Arabic and English. I don't call it a "translation." I just wrote it twice, from right to left and from left to right. As I claimed in the author's note, "allowing such a dialogue between the two texts is democratic, and even hopeful that East and West may meet in that crossing line between two languages."

> Back when there was no language
> they walked until sunset
> carrying red leaves
> like words to remember.
>
> - 'Tablets V'

DUNYA RECOMMENDS

An American Sunrise is a new poetry collection coming out in August 2019 by the newly appointed US Poet Laureate Joy Harjo, a Native American poet. In the early 1800s, the Mvskoke lands were taken away from the Creek Nation, and Joy Harjo's ancestors were forcibly displaced. Two hundred years later, Harjo returns to that land and tries to make a spiritual connection to it. These poems endeavor to make intimate spaces linking the personal history with the public.

AUTUMN BOOK REVIEWS

LAUREN K. ALLEYNE: HONEYFISH

Many of the poems in *Honeyfish* are dedicational, memorialising the victims of institutional racial violence. Despite a great depth of mournful anger beneath Alleyne's verse, her work has a scintillating, transcendent quality. She paints a living world of incredible colour, of subtle dynamism, to remind us that death can never be banal, to keep us from being numbed to what is always a profound tragedy: "How ruthless with beauty / the world seems".

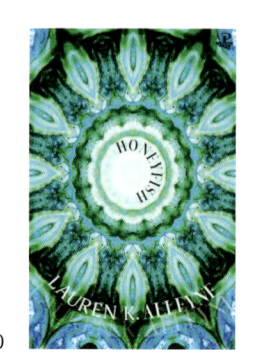

PEEPAL TREE PRESS | £9.99 | PBS PRICE £7.50

CRISPIN BEST: HELLO

Experimental, quirky and often utterly bonkers, this Faber pamphlet poet publishes his first full collection with the innovative Partus Press. Best's off-the-wall humour is an unpunctuated joy. Full of self-mocking millennial angst, and the odd avocado, a wry sadness lurks beneath: "you ask if i know / that the reason it's called gravy / is because eventually / you die". These odes to oddity cannot fail to bring a smile to your face: "o solemn wall-hung portrait of a kangaroo / o digestive biscuits in the Spring".

PARTUS PRESS | £10.99 | PBS PRICE £8.25

GUILLAUME MASSIEU: COFFEE: A POEM

The wonderful premise of a work translated from a 300-year old Latin poem about coffee does not disappoint. This bilingual edition of *Caffaeum, Carmen* will elevate any coffee table, being insightful both into historical attitudes towards the drink and the tradition of didactic poetry. Guillaume sings the praises of this "juice divine. Its nature potent 'gainst all human woes", as well as exploring its origins, the best manner in which to drink it, and numerous (spurious) health benefits.

ARC PUBLICATIONS | £9.99 | PBS PRICE £7.50

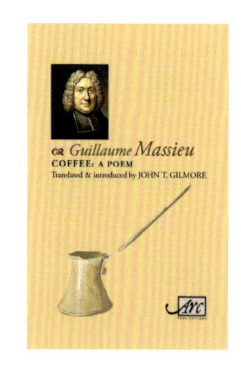

KEI MILLER: IN NEARBY BUSHES

The melodic Caribbean cadences of this Forward Prize winner cannot fail to enthrall. Kei Miller seeks the stories beneath the stories, "the understory", unravelling Jamaican place-names to question: "what do you call the thing between places". The final title sequence narrates the darker "understory" of Jamaica. This collage of poetic reportage, interspersed with extracts from the *Jamaica Star* presents a sequence of violence, ever-present "in nearby bushes".

CARCANET | £9.99 | PBS PRICE £7.50

JESSICA MOOKHERJEE: TIGRESS

Cherry blossoms, shadowed moons, paintings brought to life, love like burden and admiration intertwined. *Tigress* by Jessica Mookherjee reveals the tangles of family life in the diaspora of Bangladesh and Britain. Making narrative from the smallest of actions, this is a collection where each poem is a new adventure. Filled with the complex beauty of dark things, *Tigress* will stick with you, phrases circling for days afterwards.

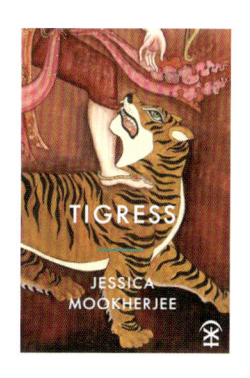

NINE ARCHES PRESS | £9.99 | PBS PRICE £7.50

KAITE O'REILLY: PERSIANS

Based on the oldest verse drama in the Western canon, Kaite O'Reilly adapts Aeschlyus' account of the Battle of Salamis and its aftermath, informed by her experiences of the Yugoslav wars, as well as Iraq and Afghanistan. Peppered with familiar jargon of the modern battlefield but holding true to the original historical setting, this dramatic addition to anti-war literature is adroit and deeply expressive, spanning both theatrical and poetic modes.

FAIR ACRE PRESS | £9.99 | PBS PRICE £7.50

AUTUMN BOOK REVIEWS

ALICE OSWALD: NOBODY

The new Oxford Professor of Poetry presents a series of water stories inspired by *The Odyssey*. This lucid sequence was originally accompanied by the watercolours of William Tillyer "whose silent shapes should be imagined in the pauses". The reader is "borne on a wave," as Oswald pools together mythic echoes of the past and the multiplicity of sea: "How does it start? The sea has endless beginnings". Ever the vivid storyteller, Oswald's poems begin and end "somewhere / in the sea".

CAPE | £10 | PBS PRICE £7.50

JACQUELINE SAPHRA: DAD, REMEMBER YOU ARE DEAD

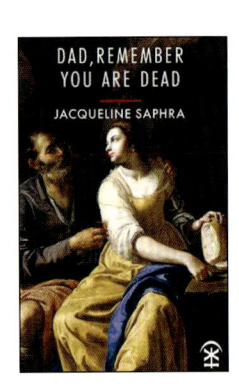

A new collection from the recent Forward Prize shortlistee. Saphra's artful, driving verse delivers a powerful retrospective on troubled and troubling family dynamics. The poet is haunted by grotesque paternal images. Accounts of irresponsible and abusive fathers from history and myth shadow an unfolding narrative of divorce and infidelity, mortality and death. Dismay and scorn, painful honesty and sheer anger burst from every page.

NINE ARCHES PRESS | £9.99 | PBS PRICE £7.50

LAURA SCOTT: SO MANY ROOMS

This debut collection by the Geoffrey Dearmer Prize-winning poet Laura Scott, spans "so many rooms" and realms with lyrical and often startling strangeness. Lucid and uncanny, these poems swim to the surface like fish "waiting for someone to tap the glass". Life is played out in a series of houses and the passage of time is measured in "years and rooms", each holding memories of their own.

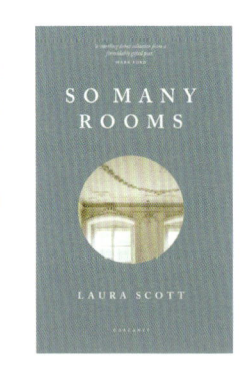

CARCANET | £9.99 | PBS PRICE £7.50

STEPHEN SEXTON: IF ALL THE WORLD AND LOVE WERE YOUNG

Stephen Sexton's Super Mario inspired debut combines poetry and Nintendo to surprising effect. Playing with real and digital worlds, this is a moving exploration of grief and nostalgia, as the young player comes to terms with his terminally ill Mother. Dreamlike worlds fade in and out of focus in this "forest of illusion", full of small green dinosaurs and retro innocence. The virtual gamer may know "the secret of infinite lives", but ultimately he must return to reality.

PENGUIN | £9.99 | PBS PRICE £7.50

EM STRANG: HORSE-MAN

Em Strang's poetry is rooted in notions of the body and of the physical, pulling down dichotomies of human/animal and material/spiritual. It conjures a strange and vital philosophy, removing boundaries between the individual and the world, foregrounding nature not as an entity separate from ourselves but as a state of being. The collection concludes with an extended sequence about the titular Horse-Man, who embodies the ideal of living in a state of immediacy and intimacy with the world about us.

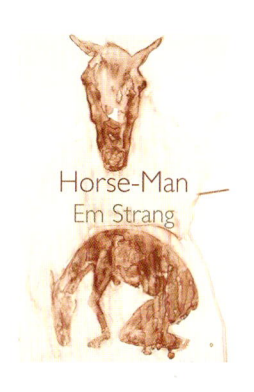

SHEARSMAN BOOKS | £9.95 | PBS PRICE £7.47

HELEN TOOKEY: CITY OF DEPARTURES

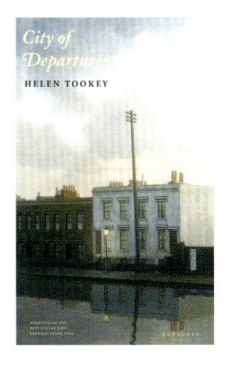

Shortlisted for the Forward Prize for Best Collection, *City of Departures* is full of "missed connections" and meanderings. These are surreal sequences, observed like "chalk dust through sunlight". We meet a woman playing a cello and a series of watchful water-ways: "Canals have always seen too much". A vast landscape of words stretches before us: "prairie is the widest word we know". Whether departing or arriving, in Copenhagen or Hamburg, these poems bring us back to where we began.

CARCANET | £9.99 | PBS PRICE £7.50

AUTUMN PAMPHLETS

FAITH LAWRENCE: SLEEPING THROUGH

Selected by Carol Ann Duffy for her Laureate's Choice series, *Sleeping Through* is a stunning debut pamphlet. Faith Lawrence's short poems employ simple language to navigate great themes. 'Delivery' introduces motherhood with surprising clarity: "clever as a key / you turned, slipped right / through and unlocked me." Reconsidering the ordinary and stripping it of any mundanity, Lawrence's poetic miniatures imbue the everyday with greater significance.

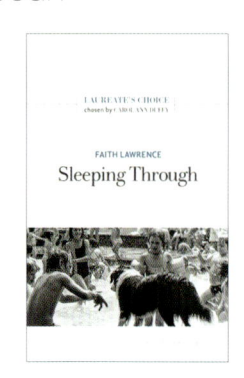

SMITH | DOORSTOP | £7.50 |

LYDIA KENNAWAY: A HISTORY OF WALKING

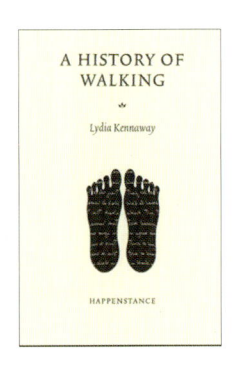

Through fairytales, historical events, and intimate portraits, *A History of Walking* takes us on journeys of tenderness and humour in sixteen poems on walking. From Little Red Riding Hood, to a mother and child separated at the border to the US, each poem is painted with gentle compassion. A master of the short sentence, Flambard Poetry Prize winner Lydia Kennaway brings us a collection brimming with honesty and wit.

HAPPENSTANCE | £5.00 |

TRISTRAM FANE SAUNDERS: WOODSONG

This striking addition to the New Poets series reminded selector Kayo Chingonyi of "poetry's capacity to tell a tale and to sing at the same time, and in so doing give us a sense of a word's arcane resonances". Drawing from the *Buile Suibhne*, an ancient Irish narrative, *Woodsong* is built upon themes of dispossession and madness, whilst remaining extremely playful. Fascinating both in content and form, this pamphlet is a lively blend of styles poetic, lyrical, dramatic and experimental.

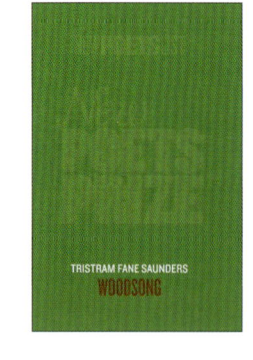

SMITH | DOORSTOP | £5.00 |

KATRINA NAOMI: TYPHOON ETIQUETTE

Inspired by an Arts Council funded trip to Japan, Katrina Naomi's fourth pamphlet crackles with all the energy of a global traveller. As Naomi explores a new country and culture, she flits between poetic forms. Japanese haikus and tankas sketch images with deft precision, while the title poem's free verse threatens to burst off the page. *Typhoon Etiquette* allows us to share moments of Naomi's journey, in all their humour, intrigue and poignancy.

VERVE POETRY PRESS | £7.50 |

RACHEL PIERCEY: DISAPPOINTING ALICE

Questions of identity are debated in this captivating pamphlet, which includes personifications of Amelia Earhart's planes and the pieces in a Guess Who? board game rendered in elegant, precise verse. Piercey is adept at drawing the reader in with suggested frivolity before sharply unravelling her metaphors into something entirely more dark and contemplative.

HAPPENSTANCE | £5.00 |

OLLIE TONG: REFLECTION MAPPING

In a variety of poetic forms, *Reflection Mapping* plays on the theme of reflections. Poems exist as echoes of subjects, of one another, of themselves, distorted like funhouse mirrors. Using concrete poetry, abstract erasure, ekphrasis, and repetition, this collection will inspire you to rediscover form. These clever poems find their meaning as much in their topography as in their words, the reader mapping their abstractions across the page.

BROKEN SLEEP BOOKS | £5.00 |

AUTUMN LISTINGS

NEW BOOKS

AUTHOR	TITLE	PUBLISHER	RRP
Lauren K. Alleyne	Honeyfish	Peepal Tree Press	£9.99
Anthony Anaxagorou	After the Formalities	Penned in the Margins	£9.99
Jericho Brown	The Tradition	Picador	£10.99
Carmen Bugan	Lilies from America: New & Selected Poems	Shearsman Books	£10.95
Jane Burn & Bob Beagrie	Remnants	Knives, Forks and Spoons	£18.00
Matthew Caley	Trawlerman's Turquoise	Bloodaxe Books	£9.95
Moya Cannon	Donegal Tarantella	Carcanet Press	£10.99
Mary Jean Chan	Flèche	Faber & Faber	£10.99
Jane Clarke	When the Tree Falls	Bloodaxe Books	£9.95
Roger Garfitt	The Action	Carcanet Press	£9.99
Paul Hawkins	Go Sift Omen	Knives, Forks and Spoons	£9.00
Sophie Herxheimer	60 Lovers to Make and Do	Henningham Family Press	£12.99
Selima Hill	I May Be Stupid But I'm Not That Stupid	Bloodaxe Books	£12.00
Lynne Hjelmgaard	A Second Whisper	Seren	£9.99
Jeremy Hooker	Word and Stone	Shearsman Books	£9.95
Peter Hughes	A Berlin Entrainment	Shearsman Books	£10.95
Chris Kinsey	From Rowan Ridge	Fair Acre Press	£9.99
Tyrone Lewis	Blackish	Burning Eye Books	£9.99
Maitreyabandhu	After Cézanne	Bloodaxe Books	£12.00
Rachel Mann	A Kingdom of Love	Carcanet Press	£9.99
Suhaiymah Manzoor-Khan	Postcolonial Banter	Verve Poetry Press	£9.99
Dunya Mikhail	In Her Feminine Sign	Carcanet Press	£10.99
Kei Miller	In Nearby Bushes	Carcanet Press	£9.99
Jessica Mookherjee	Tigress	Nine Arches Press	£9.99
Paul Muldoon	Frolic and Detour	Faber	£14.99
Mary J. Oliver	Jim Neat	Seren	£9.99
Toby Olson	Death Sentences	Shearsman Books	£9.95
Mary O'Malley	Gaudent Angeli	Carcanet Press	£9.99
Kaite O'Reilly	Persians	Fair Acre Press	£9.99
Alice Oswald	Nobody	Jonathan Cape	£10.00
Jeremy Over	Fur Coats in Tahiti	Carcanet Press	£9.99
Ness Owen	Mamiaith	Arachne Press	£8.99
Lars Palm	4 Long	Knives, Forks and Spoons	£8.00
Gareth Prior	Ibant Obscuri	Knives, Forks and Spoons	£8.00
Nisha Ramayya	States of the Body Produced by Love	Lingua Ignota	£11.99
Simon Rennie	Adverse Camber	Knives, Forks and Spoons	£10.00
Roger Robinson	A Portable Paradise	Peepal Tree Press	£9.99
Evrah Rose	Unspoken	Verve Poetry Press	£9.99
Jacqueline Saphra	Dad, Remember You Are Dead	Nine Arches Press	£9.99
Laura Scott	So Many Rooms	Carcanet Press	£9.99
Seni Seneviratne	Unknown Soldier	Peepal Tree Press	£9.99
Stephen Sexton	If All the World and Love Were Young	Penguin	£9.99
Peter Sirr	The Gravity Wave	The Gallery Press	£10.50
Em Strang	Horse-Man	Shearsman Books	£9.95
Helen Tookey	City of Departures	Carcanet Press	£9.99
David Wilson	The Equilibrium Line	Smith|Doorstop	£9.95

TRANSLATIONS

AUTHOR	TITLE	PUBLISHER	RRP
Jean Boase-Beier (ed.)	Poetry of the Holocaust	Arc Publications	£13.99
Manuel Forcano, Trans. Anna Crowe	Maps of Desire	Arc Publications	£11.99
Stein Mehren, Trans. Agnes Langeland	To the Outermost Stars	Arc Publications	£10.99

PAMPHLETS

AUTHOR	TITLE	PUBLISHER	RRP
Margaret Adkins	Mingled Space	V. Press	£6.50
Fentham Andrew	Hunglish	Broken Sleep Books	£7.00
Nick Blundell	Full blown orphan	Half Moon Books	£7.00
Andy Brown	Casket	Shearsman Books	£6.50
John-Paul Burns	The Minute & The Train	Poetry Salzburg	£6.00
Joe Carrick-Varty	Somewhere Far	Smith|Doorstop	£5.00
Antony Christie	The Archaeologist's Daughter	Wayleave Press	£5.00
Jane Clarke	All the Way Home	Smith|Doorstop	£6.00
Conor Cleary	Priced Out	The Emma Press	£6.50
Thirza Clout	Aunts Come Armed with Welsh Cakes	Smith|Doorstop	£7.50
G W Colkitto	Brantwood	Cinnamon Press	£4.99
Kelvin Corcoran	Below This Level	Shearsman Books	£6.50
Emily Cotterill	The Day of the Flying Ants	Smith|Doorstop	£7.50
Tom Cowin	When stood in occasional place	Broken Sleep Books	£5.00
Claire Crowther	Knithoard	HappenStance Press	£5.00
Tristram Fane Saunders	Woodsong	Smith|Doorstop	£5.00
SJ Fowler	I stand alone by the Devils...	Broken Sleep Books	£5.00
Jasmine Gardosi	Hurtz	Verve Poetry Press	£7.50
Victoria Gatehouse	The Mechanics of Love	Smith|Doorstop	£7.50
Anne Gill	Raft	Bad Betty Press	£6.00
Linda Goulden	Speaking Parts	Half Moon Books	£7.00
Kevein Holloway	Out of Place	Half Moon Books	£7.00
Elisabeth Horan	Bad Mommy Stay Mommy	Fly on the Wall Press	£6.99
Elisabeth Horan & Anne Walsh Donnelly	The Woman With An Owl Tattoo	Fly on the Wall Press	£6.99
Zoë Siobhan Howarth Lowe	Love is the way bark grows	Half Moon Books	£7.00
Antonia Jade King	She Too Is a Sailor	Bad Betty Press	£6.00
Sonia Jarema	Inside the Blue House	Palewell Press	£6.90
Emma Jeremy	Safety Behaviour	Smith|Doorstop	£5.00
Nick Jones	Still Life	Cinnamon Press	£6.99
Lydia Kennaway	A History of Walking	HappenStance Press	£5.00
Faith Lawrence	Sleeping Through	Smith|Doorstop	£7.50
Natalie Linh Bolderston	The Protection of Ghosts	V. Press	£6.50
Scott McKendry	Curfuffle	The Lifeboat	£6.50
Katrina Naomi	Typhoon Etiquette	Verve Poetry Press	£7.50
Helena Nelson	Branded	Red Squirrel Press	£6.00
Caitlin Newby	Ceremony	The Lifeboat	£6.50
Ben Norris	Some Ending	Verve Poetry Press	£7.50
Eugene Ostashevsky	The Feeling Sonnets	clinic	£5.00
Rachel Piercey	Disappointing Alice	HappenStance Press	£5.00
Colin Pink	The Ventriloquist Dummy's Lament	Against the Grain	£10.00
Alan Stanley Prout	Then become	Half Moon Books	£7.00
Belinda Rimmer	Touching Sharks in Monaco	Indigo Dreams	£6.00
Bethany Rivers	The sea refuses no river	Fly on the Wall Press	£6.99
Lenni Sanders	Poacher	The Emma Press	£6.50
Adham Smart	Yes Yes Mouth	Valley Press	£7.99
Jeffery Sugarman	Dear Friend(s)	The Emma Press	£6.50
Ollie Tong	Reflection Mapping	Broken Sleep Books	£5.00
Becky Varley-Winter	Heroines: On the Blue Peninsula	V. Press	£6.50
U. G. Világos	Collected Experimentalisms: 1989-1992	Broken Sleep Books	£5.00
Dawn Watson	The Stack of Owls is Getting Higher	The Emma Press	£6.50
Django Wylie	New and Selected Heartbreaks	Indigo Dreams	£6.00
Warda Yassin	Tea with Cardamom	Smith|Doorstop	£5.00

BOOK CLUB OFFER

Forward Prizes for Poetry

Poetry Book Society

10 Books & Reading Notes ONLY £60 for PBS Members

WWW.POETRYBOOKS.CO.UK